housebeautiful

SENSATIONAL work spaces

The Editors of House Beautiful Magazine

hearst books

A Division of Sterling Publishing Co., Inc.
New York

Copyright © 2002 by Hearst Communications, Inc.

Library of Congress Cataloging-in-Publication Data

Sensational work spaces / text by the editors of House beautiful magazine.
p. cm.

At head of title: House beautiful.
Includes index.
ISBN 1-58816-188-9
1. Home offices—United States—Design and construction. 2. Office decoration—
United States. I. House beautiful.

NK2195.O4 S46 2002
747.7'3—dc21

2002025046

10 9 8 7 6 5 4 3 2 1

Published by Hearst Books,
A Division of Sterling Publishing Company, Inc.
387 Park Avenue South, New York, N.Y. 10016

House Beautiful and Hearst Books are trademarks owned by
Hearst Magazines Property, Inc., in USA, and Hearst Communications, Inc., in Canada.

www.housebeautiful.com

Distributed in Canada by Sterling Publishing
c/o Canadian Manda Group, One Atlantic Avenue, Suite 105
Toronto, Ontario, Canada M6K 3E7
Distributed in Australia by Capricorn Link (Australia) Pty. Ltd.
P.O. Box 704, Windsor, NSW 2756 Australia

Edited by Paula Rackow

Printed in China

ISBN 1-58816-188-9

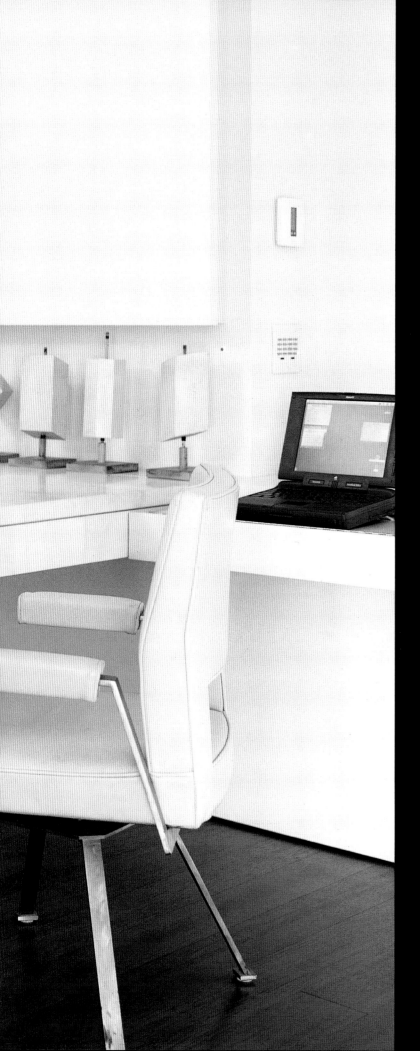

Contents

Introduction

The home office is not really a new idea. Once man had made the transition from toiling over stone tablets to writing on stationary desks, the place he usually preferred for work or contemplation was his home. The Renaissance nobleman had his *studiolo,* the captain of industry his study, the merchant his fall-front desk in the parlor. It was only after the Industrial Revolution that business began moving into what became the corporate office environments most of us know. Even then, working at home never disappeared entirely. As long as there were overloaded desks and last-minute crises, people continued to take work home from the office. But in the past decade or so, they've been taking home the office itself.

The home office phenomenon began in the postwar business boom of the 1950s and 1960s, accelerating as more women joined the workforce. In recent years, a more relaxed attitude toward work, and the desire of working parents to spend more time with their families, have spurred this trend. New technology has made it easy, with personal computers, e-mail, pagers, and teleconferencing revolutionizing the way we work. Personal computers and storage discs have replaced bulky filing cabinets, and advanced communications have made possible the office in a briefcase—or even in the palm of your hand.

So, although home was once a place to escape the tensions of the office—and sometimes vice versa—the walls between the two are coming down. As the nine-to-five workday gives way to flex-time schedules, the home can serve as an adjunct office or the two can share a single location. According to recent estimates, the number of people who work at home, occasionally or daily, is increasing at almost geometric rates. More than 20 percent of all Americans work at home, and more than 80 percent of Americans, of all ages and occupations, maintain some form of home office. This sea change has transformed the home office from a convenience into a fundamental element of modern life, a must-have feature in almost every type of residence. It can be anything from a shelf in a corner of the kitchen to a full-scale office requiring its own room. For most people, it's something in between.

The following pages illustrate a series of rooms or parts of rooms, all with very different styles, features, and arrangements. In each case, the occupants and their designers put individual needs and personalities into play to create comfortable work areas in the places where they live. None of these is the ideal home office—there is probably no such thing—but one just may suit your own particular space, work habits, and personal taste. Whether your strategy is to work in private in a converted closet or take over a sideboard in the dining room, you're sure to discover ideas for a work space that will be practical, attractive—and very much like home.

sensational work spaces

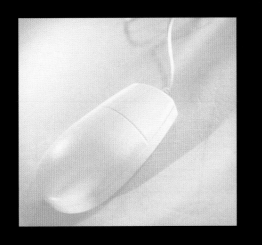

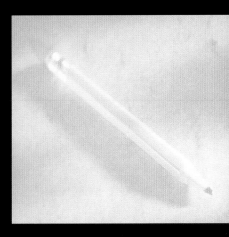

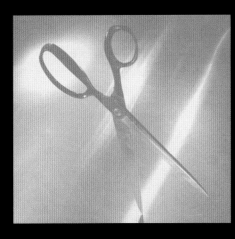

A Space of One's Own

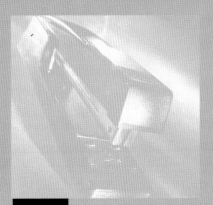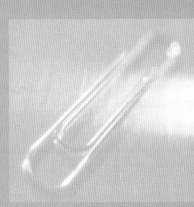

T he home office can be the best possible place to
work—or the worst. Ideally, it allows you to conduct your business in a space designed to your specifications, with everything
you need and everything you want close at hand. It can also
be a headache: no colleagues to chat with, no assistants for
backup, and more distractions than would ever exist in a "real"
office. The chatty office worker or the tiresome phone conversation is replaced by the child demanding attention, the dog
whining for a walk, or the boisterous after-school gathering of
teenagers. There are many impediments to toiling in peace and
quiet in a home shared with others; the trend to multitasking
notwithstanding, there's nothing more frustrating or less productive than trying to work amid interruptions by deliverymen,
spouses, or the sounds of video games or TV. To overcome

In the high-ceilinged ground-floor room of this sophisticated New York town house (opposite), decorator Sharon Simonaire used a dramatically curving desk by early modernist
Charlotte Perriand as a focal point, placing it at one end of the narrow, multipurpose
space to catch the light from tall, street-facing windows. The table's sweeping surface
provides a generous area for the fashion photographer–owner to spread out her work,
while stacks of reference books are within easy reach on shelves nearby. In these stylish surroundings, the desk doubles as a buffet table for casual entertaining.

Getting Started

To define your needs, answer these
five key questions:

1. **How will you use the home office?** Examine your
typical workday and list each specific activity.

2. **How often will you work at home?** Decide
whether you need a permanent arrangement or a work
space that can be set up on demand.

3. **At what time of day or night will you be working?**
Don't place your office in playrooms, bedrooms, or
other areas that may be in use when you need them.

4. **How much space will you need?** Consider
everything your home office will require, including
equipment and storage.

5. **What is your comfort level?** Think about light,
noise, temperature, privacy, ambience—whatever will
make you feel at home in your home office.

Can an office morph into a dining room at a moment's
notice? The owner of this well-bred North Carolina farm country home
needed both work space and a second dining table, but barely had
room for either one.

The solution was this sleek updated variation on a Colonial gateleg
table, which fits snugly against the wall in a corner. In this secluded
spot it serves as a day-to-day desktop, but when company comes
the drop leaf can be opened up, making a second dining table. The
palomino tones of polished ash furniture are a graceful and unexpected complement to the rough fieldstone walls and pine plank floor. A
sleek standing lamp is close at hand, and papers are neatly stacked
in file boxes in the rolling shelf unit that doubles as a wall divider (overleaf).

overcome such everyday obstacles, some degree of privacy is
absolutely essential. Even if you live alone, it's wise to separate—visually, if not literally—your work area from your home
life. Otherwise, work is apt to take over, and you'll find yourself compulsively drawn deskward when you'd rather be doing
something else . . . or when family demands should take precedence over work. Then there's the opposite problem: If your
office space is not sufficiently separated, the urge to clean or
snack or pick up that novel you've been enjoying—to do anything but work—may prove overwhelming.

Despite such impediments, every year more of us are
deciding that the advantages of a home office—the potential
tax benefits (your accountant will tell you what they are in
your particular case), the savings on commuting time and
expense (and possibly your wardrobe), and the sheer satisfaction of being able to work at your own pace, on a schedule you
choose—outweigh its inconveniences.

Any home office should meet four critical requirements:
convenient location, the right amount of space, the necessary
equipment, and pleasant ambience. In the real world, however,
these almost never coexist. Space, layout, and budget constraints may result in an office that falls somewhat short of the
ideal. But it's possible to come close—or at least to try. Even
lacking the first two essentials, good planning and a willingness
to compromise can help create a functional, comfortable home
office. Once organized, it can be decorated as attractively as any
other area of your home.

he home office can be the best possible place to work—or the worst. Ideally, it allows you to conduct your business in a space designed to your specifications, with everything you need and everything you want close at hand. It can also be a headache: no colleagues to gossip with, no assistants for backup, and more distractions than would ever exist in a "real" office. The chatty office worker or the tiresome phone conversation is replaced by the child demanding attention, the dog whining for a walk, or the boisterous after-school gathering of teenagers. There are many impediments to toiling in peace and quiet in a home shared with others; the trend toward multitasking notwithstanding, there's nothing more frustrating or less productive than trying to work amid interruptions by deliverymen, spouses, or the sounds of video games or TV. To overcome such everyday obstacles, some degree of privacy is absolutely essential. Even if you live alone, it's wise to separate—visually, if not literally—your work area from your home life. Otherwise, work is apt to take over, and you'll find yourself compulsively drawn deskward when you'd rather be doing something else . . . or when family demands should take precedence over work. Then there's the opposite problem: If your office space is not sufficiently separated, the urge to clean or snack or pick up that novel you've been enjoying—to do anything but work—may prove overwhelming.

Despite such impediments, every year more of us are deciding that the advantages of a home office—the potential tax benefits (your accountant will tell you what they are in

Peaceful coexistence was the goal for designer Noel Jeffrey when he was asked to turn a long narrow room in a spacious New York City apartment into a versatile space that could do triple duty as library, entertainment center, and home office. But how do you design a room that's at once relaxing and hard working?

Solution Jeffrey arranged an away-from-the-wall seating area to visually separate work and recreational areas. Built-in bookcases were expanded vertically for additional shelving and to discreetly house the television, sound system, and storage drawers. Antique library steps added charm as well as access to the top bookshelves. To unify the areas of work and relaxation, the owners placed fine ceramic and metal objects throughout, adding their personal stamp.

Works well The overscale Georgian writing table (opposite) is paired with matching armchairs, permitting the owners to work from either side—or in tandem.

Could a rundown Pasadena cottage become a modern, light-filled work space for two people? California designer Matthew White wanted an office that felt like a "home away from home." The trick was to create the openness of contemporary design without losing the charm and warmth of the original structure.

Solution White created a striking angular space (opposite and overleaf) framed by a low dividing wall that separates it from his assistant's office. An oversized window adds to the contemporary look and floods the room with light. Result, a modern office that feels more like a sunroom. The window seat bay, original beams, fireplaces, and double doors leading to a garden add cozy touches.

Works well Design project photos are held in place by crisscrossed ribbons, at once useful yet evocative of earlier times.

the office. Don't forget files, shelves, and other storage areas, and extra space for meetings or employees.

Finally, what about personal needs? Some people crave natural light; some can't work without music. You may be heat or cold sensitive or need quick, easy access to beverages or snacks. Think about your own idiosyncrasies and plan for them.

With the answers to these questions in mind, you're ready to make a realistic evaluation of your available space. Go through every part of your home and explore the possibilities—space that can go solo, space that can be shared, space you can create from scratch. You may be one of the happy few who have the luxury of a separate office, but most likely your work will share precious square footage with other activities. The challenge is to find a congenial partnership that makes the best possible use of space without shortchanging any of its uses—or users. In accommodating both living and working, the home office must balance the two, yet keep them apart. Office conversation at dinnertime is one thing—scattered papers on the table is another, and an altogether undesirable one. Equally important, you should be able to switch the area's functions without elaborate reconfiguration.

It's a knotty problem, but anyone who's solved it will probably tell you that the results are worth the effort. In a well-equipped and attractively decorated home office, you can have the best of both worlds: the satisfaction of a day's work done in comfortable surroundings and, when the workday is over and colleagues begin the tedious trip back home, the not-so-guilty pleasure of already being there.

A welcoming air and the sumptuousness of a beautifully furnished home were what a busy Los Angeles executive wanted when this floor-through apartment was transformed into work space. For designer Thomas Beeton the challenge was a formidable one—how to fit a massive black desk, file drawers, and oversized conference table into the space while maintaining the desired warm, homelike mood.

Solution Beeton started by painting the conference room walls a lush umber and the office a brilliant red. These bold, hardly traditional office colors instantly created the requisite warmth and are strong enough to keep the furniture from dominating. The neoclassical-style mantel and molding inject just the right elegant note in the parlor, and simple window blinds maintain the overall contemporary look of the room. In the office, sculptural ebony lamps, a curved Harvey Probber guest chair, and other shapely accessories soften the severity of the angular furniture.

Works well For pinning up presentations, Beeton covered one wall of the office with woven matting, turning it into a giant but handsome tackboard.

Why it works Color can create mood and help to blend in imposing furniture or architectural features. Offices don't have to be white.

How could an elegant central hall with 24-foot ceilings possibly provide work space while still functioning as the formal entrance to this 1784 manor house in St. Croix? With its grand architectural framework this imposing room seemed an unlikely backdrop for a home office. But the owner, an inveterate preservationist, was undaunted.

Solution To match the grandeur of the room, a magnificent American Chippendale mahogany desk-bureau with a fall front writing surface was chosen. However, the desk is also hard working, with convenient cubbyholes and deep drawers. A table at the end of the room offers more space for spreading out books and papers.

Works well Instead of lamps and sundry office equipment, the space above the desk is occupied by a stunning American Empire gilt mirror. Together, desk and mirror make a striking decorative statement, camouflaging their workaday role.

Why it works By coordinating the furnishings correctly, you can create a home office in almost any room with sufficient space.

The boundaries between inside and outside are temptingly porous in this room perched on a woodsy hillside in the San Francisco bay area (right). Designer Tony Cantalini had to create a space that could be transformed from office to dining room without sacrificing the functionality of either—or interfering with the open feel of the architecture.

Solution Cantalini devised a multipurpose curving credenza of warm cherry with drawers that hold both work files and food serving accessories. Doubling as a desk and sideboard, its granite top is easy to clean and heat resistant as well. Some of the most practical touches are unseen (above). The printer is concealed in a slide-away compartment, and wires run into stainless steel grommets to hide beneath the countertop. The handsome Philippe Starck chairs are as appropriate for dinner guests as they are deskside.

Why it works In addition to thinking about the size, shape, and location of your office furniture, consider the materials as well. Here multi-functional granite is what allows this room to gracefully accommodate two functions—work and dining.

Not your ordinary home office, this capacious loft space in New York's Soho neighborhood serves as an artist's studio, providing everything the owner requires to create her paintings, collages, and sculptures (left). Although aesthetics take a backseat to efficiency, well-proportioned furnishings and exuberant applications of bright red—her favorite color—make for an appealing ambience in what might otherwise be an austere space. The most striking decorative statements are the oversize figures on structural columns and centered on one wall. Anchoring the studio, a grand-scale rolling worktable adjusts to several heights. Around the perimeter, storage units provide both shallow and deep storage drawers, file space, and countertops (above). Chairs are spare and simple, and natural lighting is supplemented by ceiling-mounted fixtures. Finished work or works in progress are the only other decoration in the room—and all it needs.

As wide open as the Texas prairie that surrounds it, this house is virtually one loft-like room. The owner makes most of his art in a studio separated by a breezeway, but he needed a spot where he could keep his paperwork and office equipment.

Solution Architect Max Levy installed a series of handsome custom-built-in maple storage units to define different spaces without walling them in. Since the desk is directly opposite the bed, anything unsightly or distracting is concealed in touch-latch cabinets above and generous file drawers beneath; the accompanying chair is small in scale and unobtrusive. The lamps are mounted neatly over the desktop—not that they get much use during the day, when ambient light pours in through a large triangular skylight, fitted with a shade to subdue the strong Texas sun.

Works well The divider that holds the desk doesn't quite reach the ceiling. As a result, the piece seems to float in the light-filled space, adding to the feeling of openness.

This well-equipped corner office needed enough style to stand up to its punchy orange, white, and black surroundings (left).

Solution Instead of disguising the work space, designers Agnes Bourne and Geoffrey de Sousa showed off its function, choosing a modular mahogany worktable and black ash open bookcases (above). The front apron of the curved counter swings down to hold a computer keyboard, but the monitor stands front and center. The bright graphic rug is attractively angled to define the living space.

Works well The witty numerical drawer pulls on the ash cabinets make a bold decorative statement—as if to say we're here, we're functional, there's nothing to hide.

An inviting den can also be a fully functioning office. The sleek, glass-top table, whimsical lamp, and statuesque sconces fit in neatly with the architect-owner's art collection and iconic chairs by Le Corbusier, Rietveld, and Mackintosh. Walls that stop short of the ceiling and broad, open doorways heighten the effect of space to spare in this Arizona home. At the window wall, a chest has shallow drawers for blueprints, and cantilevered shelves hold design and architecture books. A pillow-strewn couch at one end and well-lighted chaise longue at the other stand ready for either study or relaxation at the end of the workday.

The extraordinary New Haven home of architect Peter de Bretteville and his wife, Sheila, a graphic designer, was reclaimed from an abandoned water-storage tank. De Bretteville transformed the 50-foot-by-25-foot drum-shape space, reconfiguring it into a two-story interior that includes offices, drafting studio, and a library with more than 500 linear feet of books (both husband and wife are professors at Yale University). The living room sits on the other side of a low wall from the soaring, two-story library that comprises the core of the building (opposite). A steel stairway leads to the second floor. The top shelves, reserved for seldom-needed volumes such as old children's books, are reached by a steel ladder that's kept out of sight. Behind the library, the north-lit studio-work area is equipped with drafting tables (right), flanked by his-and-her private offices (not shown). De Bretteville designed a plywood and steel table for the library that serves equally well for research, meetings, or dining (overleaf, left). A view from the second-floor balcony (overleaf, right) shows the table ready for entertaining. The chairs are a mix of salvaged relics and flea market finds. Tall windows on the building's perimeter allow light to stream in from all sides, and industrial-style fixtures provide supplementary illumination.

Just outside his small shingle-style cottage in Sausalito, California, architect John Marsh Davis managed to find room for an office even though the area was small: a mere 20 feet long by 8 feet wide. The challenge was to design an office that didn't feel claustrophobic. **Solution** The steeply angled glass roof brings in the outdoors and plenty of light, while floor to ceiling mirrors along both walls expand the space visually. The office is neatly outfitted with all the prerequisites for an architect—drafting table, tall chair, blueprint file drawers, and flexible task light.

Why it works Here, the lush flora add a lively visual touch and ensure that Davis will take time to smell the roses. Remember that you can have fun with your office.

Designers' own residences are usually the best show-cases for their work—and their work habits. In the library of the Long Island barn complex that serves as her weekend home, designer Mariette Himes Gomez wanted to brighten a space that might otherwise have been overwhelmed by the tightly packed ceiling-high bookshelves.

Solution Gomez used vividly colored vintage upholstery and fabrics to capture the eye and brighten the room. The window becomes the setting for her desk, a separate area where she does collage and watercolor painting—her preferred work away from work.

Works well The traditional tilt-top drafting table is made of wood, so it blends in perfectly with the window framing and bookshelves, allowing the bright seating arrangement to be the room's focal point.

This spanking-modern, book-lined area was designed by architect Jack de Bartolo Jr. as a self-contained office suite in his Arizona home. Generously proportioned, the space divides in two: an open area with a granite table that allows for meetings with colleagues as well as room to spread out and work in good natural light, and a more private section that houses a long counter facing a bulletin-board wall of memos and memory-jogging notes. Classic Pollak executive office chairs pull up to either area, as does the ubiquitous white plastic Boby unit that holds the tools of the architect's trade. Efficient built-in and task lighting supplements the sunlight that streams through the wall of windows.

Not everyone who works at home needs a conventional desk. In a New York City town house, this stripped to the basics studio had to fit both the contemporary taste and the special requirements of the artist who uses it.

Solution A 3-foot-by-5-foot table with a laminate top and metal base provides a broad practical surface for flat painting and print-making. A pair of wall-mounted vintage chrome fixtures contribute additional light.

Works well An efficient arrangement of translucent sliding panels in acid-blackened perforated steel conceals art supplies, books, artworks, and a fax machine—without visually closing off the space.

In the study of a bachelor's Boston aerie, the burden of paperwork is lifted by dizzying views out the penthouse windows. The modest-size desk allows the owner, a real-estate developer, to look out on a skyline that he helped shape. The work surface is the same deep-stained mahogany as the paneled walls and built-in cabinetry that wrap around every room in the residence. The rich background, and its complementary palette of soft neutral tones—what Celeste Cooper, the apartment's designer, calls "Armani colors"—were chosen to suit her client's urbane taste. Maintaining the understated look, the desk is fitted with a sleek metal lamp and paired with a soigné Edward Wormley mahogany armchair.

Finding Your Niche

I t's easy to understand why more and more people go to work simply by moving from one room to another—often without even changing from robe and slippers into conventional business garb. But the home office isn't what it used to be. The card table in the corner is out of date, and so are cartons piled high in the closet. Today's home offices are well-appointed, professional, and personalized, and pulling them together can take considerable planning. Still, you can find ingenious ways to carve out usable work space in almost any room in the home. And with a bit of imagination and a why-not-try-it attitude, you can even create space where none existed.

You don't have to be a magician to reclaim footage from a furnished room—just draft vacant space into service or convert an underutilized area into one that does double duty.

Almost any corner can be pressed into service to create a home office. In this West Virginia house, architect Laura Hartman found herself in a tight spot, so she shoehorned a desk into a corner of the master-suite study. By attaching one end of the writing surface to the wall and eliminating the need for vertical supports there, she created additional room for bookshelves. The natural oak unit suits the owners' folk art collection as well as the rustic nature of the surrounding countryside. Tucked beneath an angled ladder, the work space gives the illusion of privacy, while desk-level windows banish any sense of claustrophobia.

Can a streamlined kitchen provide just enough desk space for perusing cookbooks, paying bills, or sending faxes? Designer Amanda Halstead was asked to pack every possible convenience, including a washer dryer and closed door cabinets to hide clutter in this compact New York City high-rise apartment. But where to put the desk became the question.

Solution A slip of a stool slides under the mitered corner of a countertop, instantly turning it into a minimalist workstation for writing or reading. The easy-to-clean woodgrain-laminate countertops stand up to the demands of both scribe and chef.

Works well Neatly displayed on shallow open shelves, dinnerware and appliances gain stature as sculptural objects, yet are still easily reached.

Think multitasking: What about . . . the formal dining room that's gathering cobwebs when you're not throwing dinner parties? the dressing table where you apply makeup every morning? the library table that's seen more of your glass collection than books? the hulking entertainment unit that dwarfs the equipment in it? the little-used pantry off the kitchen? And think creatively: Can you use that walk-in closet (and store its contents elsewhere)? that useless hallway with its dead-end wall? that bay window, attic alcove, dormer niche, or space beneath the stairs? Some solutions might involve construction—finishing the attic, converting the garage or basement, enclosing a porch or terrace (though this generally requires adding heating and air-conditioning), or even building on an additional room. In a high-ceilinged apartment, consider adding a loft or overhead gallery just wide enough to hold a desk, chair, and file cabinets.

Your strategy will depend on your particular requirements. That cute little alcove in the den won't do if you need yards of desktop, and the entry foyer may be a problem if it lacks space for files. Privacy may be an impossible dream in a bedroom shared with someone else, and if you need quiet, it's a good idea to avoid kitchens or entrance halls, usually the busiest areas of any home. (Conversely, you'll also want to place an office with a constantly ringing phone out of earshot.) Finally, if your work is paper-intensive, it's inconvenient to work in the living room or any other area that must be cleared when you're finished for the day. Once you've weighed the can't-live-withouts and the

what's-availables, you can make an educated decision and select the area that fulfills most, if not all, of your needs.

Once you've claimed your territory, you should plan the arrangement of your space. Don't skip this step! Get out your tape measure and make a floor plan, complete with measurements. Even a casual sketch will prevent you from purchasing a desk that's too large or shelves that aren't tall or deep enough. Remember, not all your furniture has to go against the wall. One way to gain space in a well-proportioned room is to pull the seating arrangement toward the center, leaving walls free for bookshelves, storage units, and the work space you need. (If you don't intend to move soon, consider built-ins—they're a great way to maximize your space, and the shelves can be configured precisely to your needs.) If there's flexibility in the space you've chosen, experiment with layouts: the conventional L-shape space, the more generous U, or perhaps a pair of parallel work surfaces with a chair that swivels between them.

Don't forget to plan for at least one degree of separation, enough to give you the illusion of distance, both psychological and physical—a decorative screen, a freestanding bookcase, or an area rug, for example. Sometimes facing furniture in a different direction will do the trick. Some sort of enclosure or camouflage is especially handy if you can't (or don't want to) clear off the desk between working sessions. (It can also keep you from being reminded of unfinished business.)

Now you're ready to furnish the workstation—or to have it designed for you. Leave extras such as decorative

HOME / WORK

Setting Up Shop
Follow these steps for a foolproof strategy:

- **Locate:** Find a space you're not using, space you can double up, space you can build.

- **Allocate:** Devise a floor plan to make sure the space isn't bigger in your imagination than it is in real life.

- **Separate:** Create a barrier between office and home, even if it's only a visual one.

- **Decorate:** You have nobody to please but yourself, so choose your favorite colors and a style that suits your taste.

- **Organize:** Having a place for everything lets you work more efficiently.

In a 1950s-style Palm Springs, California, ranch house, three retro-loving New Yorkers furnished a getaway retreat with vintage furnishings and lots of lively color. But even a vacation house sometimes needs a place for occasional work, so the owners created an office space in a bedroom niche where a closet used to be. Still, the cantilevered work surface, which seems to hover like a flying saucer, is ample enough for a laptop and assorted accessories and beautiful enough to fit in with its space-age surroundings.

With prized beachfront property, square footage is at a premium. So architect Steven Ehrlich made every inch count when adapting this Santa Monica, California, residence to suit his clients' work-at-home needs. Devoting most of the interior to essential living and entertaining areas, he squeezed in a study by widening a second-floor mezzanine and setting a narrow, glass-top desk against the railing. Low filing cabinets behind it provide an additional work surface when needed. A slim, adjustable task light and minimalist office chair fit the scale and style of the space. Best of all, it's a room with a view—the pounding Pacific.

lamps, wastebaskets, and storage trolleys for last—once they're in place, things often look bigger and take up more space than you expect.

The final step, and the most enjoyable one, is decorating your office to suit your taste. When picking colors, think lively, not muted: crisp white, sky blue, sunny yellow, even wakeup red. Pastels are pretty, but a palette that's too subdued may lull you into languor instead of stimulating you to get into gear. And keep things simple: A single, striking work of art is less distracting than an arrangement of small objects—and much easier to keep clean. If your office is part of an existing room, then it should, of course, be compatible with the decor.

Whatever your work habits and design preferences, you'll have to get organized. Keep each aspect of your life in its place and ensure that office disarray doesn't spill over into the rest of your home. File your papers when you're not working; documents left scattered on the desk are not only unsightly, they're all too accessible.

Some of these challenges may seem insurmountable, but designers face and conquer them almost every day. The photographs in this section show work-at-home spaces conjured from a tremendous range of homes, each with its own constellation of opportunities and limitations. As you explore these canny creations by some of the country's most ingenious designers, you're sure to find a solution to your own spatial squeeze.

When all that's required is a surface for making lists or dropping mail, the space just inside an entrance will do. Adding English country-cottage charm to an eighteenth-century Connecticut house (opposite), the owners placed an old desk at right angles to a staircase wall to create an alcove office that's cleverly unconstricted. Similarly, the useless space beside the stairway of another country home was transformed into a mini-office (above).

Making it work To help fit your office into your home, accessorize with non-traditional office accessories such as an antique mirror or a chair (left), or a handsome picture arrangement and lamp (above).

In a structure that's as much about windows as walls, the architect of this bi-level New Mexico home, David Lake of Lake/Flato, didn't want to distract from the magnificent views. Yet his clients needed a study.

Solution The cantilevered walkway that passes over a below-grade greenhouse offered the opening. Lake lined the wall, which is outside the bedroom, with bookcases and set a steel table desk and office-issue swivel chair just in front. His careful placement left the sweeping views intact and the daylight streaming through.

Works well The simple desk was chosen to blend in. Tubular steel legs mimic the guard rail, while the white surface fits in seamlessly with the white walls.

In a flat that's short on space, even a hallway can be something more. Turnbull Griffin Haesloop reconfigured a San Francisco apartment (above), turning a hall into a guest room—the sofa bed is out of view—and study. Built-in cherry shelves and storage create a warm atmosphere, and a drop-leaf desk can be transformed into a dressing table. In a small Manhattan apartment (opposite), a design-savvy world traveler created the look of a book-lined study with trompe l'oeil wallpaper that visually stretches the space.

There's no such thing as "dead space." Stretching the boundaries of convention in a Connecticut weekend house (above), designer T. Keller Donovan perched a just-large-enough desk perpendicular to bookcases at the end of a landing. Chairs on both sides allow the owners to do their letter writing or household accounts together. In a more open but equally narrow setting (opposite), architect Robert Dripps borrowed one end of the breeze-way that connects two wings of his loftlike Virginia home for the same purpose. Corner windows usher nature into the bright white surroundings.

An **appealing entry-foyer** seemed the logical spot for a workstation in the Los Angeles home of designer Kate Stamps. But how would a work desk fit in with its stately surroundings?

Solution This taller-than-most chest with a drop-lid writing surface proved to be ideal. An eighteenth-century mahogany treasure, the imposing piece more than measured up to its glamorous setting. Fitting accompaniments include a tiny lamp, a congenial mix of chairs in seventeenth- and nineteenth-century styles, and selections from Stamp's creamware collection. Even the wastebasket, painted to suggest a nineteenth-century pastoral scene, makes a decorative contribution to the attractive vignette.

Keep in mind Your work desk does not necessarily have to be hidden or minimized. Consider buying an important piece of furniture and making it the star of your room.

Celebrated for his ingenuity as well as his mastery of the modern vernacular, Italian designer Vico Magistretti fashioned work spaces for almost every room in his spacious Milan apartment. The furnishings include many familiar pieces created by the prolific master over his five-decade career. In the living room (left, above), a sweeping desk faces Magistretti's daybed and sofa, effectively dividing the work and social areas. At one end of his bedroom (left, below), his witty adjustable screw-base desk is paired with Arne Jacobsen's classic Ant chair. The library (opposite) is the repository of various ethnic crafts as well as the cherished oak desk belonging to his father. The tufted-leather ottoman is identical to the one in the living room.

This sleek dining room in an elegant Paris flat hardly seemed the likely place for a home office. There were no convenient nooks or crannies and the room was used frequently for dinner parties. **Solution** French designer Christian Liaigre created a modern armoire that hides a full-scale home office behind finely veneered doors (above). Covered in a pale mahogany that flatters the room's neutral color scheme, the unit takes up almost an entire wall. It stops several inches short of the ceiling to suggest more space beyond, yet it's shallow enough not to intrude into the room. When the doors are fully opened, a drop shelf becomes a desk (left). Indirect lighting is built in, and full-width shelves hold file-storage boxes. With the doors closed, the dining room can play host to formal dinners without revealing its workaday role.

Now you see it, now you don't: A bit of imagination (and meticulous measuring) can turn a wasted alcove into a storage or work area. To fill the niche that once held a Murphy bed, the owner of this small New York apartment found an enormous seventeenth-century German cupboard that was just the right size (left, above) and replaced its interior fittings with custom housing for a home entertainment system, laptop, and peripherals (left, below). Had he needed one here, a desk would have been an easy inclusion. In the book-lined entry of the same apartment, a drop-lid antique desk fits neatly into a shelf-flanked alcove (opposite). Beyond it, a decorative carpet hung from the celing conceals the entrance, rotating in place when the door is opened. The cozy, cluttered look of the space belies the careful planning that made it possible.

If home-office needs are relatively modest, even a stripped-down modern room can accommodate sufficient desk space. In a renovated 1920s New York City apartment (above), designer Ken Foreman wedged a work area into a tiny bedroom's window alcove—just enough room for a computer, with a mini-storage area recessed into the corner beam. Architect Lee S. Mindel maxed out tight space in a New York loft (opposite) with a longish, narrow desk, ceiling-high bookshelves, and a skinny Arne Jacobsen chair.

Keep in mind Eliminate clutter in order to retain a spare look and prevent the office from imposing on the rest of the room.

Barely large enough to fit a desk, this compact corner has the expansive feel of an executive office, thanks to the unobstructed waterfront view. Contributing to the bright, airy effect are timeless Eames steel-frame pieces that are equal parts void and solid: the desk with its birch top and painted hardboard drawer and accent panel, and the plywood and hardboard storage unit. The latter acts as a porous screen that separates the work area from the larger space. A small desk lamp and built-in fixtures overhead supplement the abundant natural light.

A room that's simple and unfussy needn't be modern. Witness the compact living and working quarters designed by William Hodgins for his own condominium in Boston's Ritz-Carlton Hotel. Condensing the furnishings and accessories from a much larger home, Hodgins put together a room that's full of objects yet never seems crowded. He achieved the airy effect by enveloping the surround in white and confining the large-scale furniture—the gray-painted partner's desk and white upholstered seating (above)—to light tones. Arranging the furniture along the floor grid of 22-inch square tiles also added to the sense of order (right). Carefully editing his extensive collections of bronzes and faience, many of them Asian, the designer displays them in custom-built shelving above a series of closed cabinets that conceal files. A small pull-up unit behind the desk keeps stationery close at hand.

Anyone who complains about lack of space should take this example to heart. Reconfiguring a New York City apartment, Cynthia Butler of Insight Design had to fit everything the owner needed, including capacious storage and work space, into just 700 square feet.

Solution Double-duty furnishings proved the key to transforming the living room into a versatile home entertainment center, office, and small dining area (left). The custom-made wall unit of metal, wood, and glass offered maximum storage and created a small nook to the right that was neatly filled by a desk and computer. The glass-topped flat-file cabinet holds a photography collection and also serves as a movable coffee table. Storage is tucked behind the radiator covers on either side of the heating units. What appears to be a wall of exterior windows behind the sofa are actually patterned glass doors that can pivot in place to open to the bedroom beyond.

Pristine white walls and candy-color Pierre Paulin seating lend a lighthearted look to this Paris apartment. In keeping with the breezy appearance, the essentials of a home office are enclosed in an all-in-one portable unit designed by Christian Biecher. Set into the corner of the living room, it takes up no more space than an ordinary bookcase but handily holds computer, keyboard shelf, fax machine, and plenty of papers—attractively concealed in colorful file-storage boxes. Equally compact, the quirky backless chair is ergonomically designed for seating comfort.

An attic can be turned into a delightful retreat that combines guest room and work space. The trick is decorating so that the space provides both a welcoming refuge for visitors and the working necessities for the owner.

Solution In this long and narrow New York town house, designers Katherine McCallum and Priscilla Ullmann began with a twig-patterned wallpaper that minimizes the jogs and angles of the room. A venerable drop-lid secretary stands splendidly along the major wall (right), providing handy cubbyholes and drawers, while bookshelves are tucked under the slanted ceiling. A charming mix of old furniture, framed prints, and throw pillows handsomely accomplish the task of turning this under-the-eaves room into a warm, relaxing spot for guests.

Works well A small table and chairs (above) provide the perfect spot for collaborations or cozy breakfasts à deux.

Can a small home office be glamorous? The owner of the apartment at left possessed a taste for simplicity and an eye for drama but was short on space.

Solution Designer Brian Stoner found an opportunity to create an office in the otherwise useless L-shape entry. He designed a strictly business built-in desk to fit precisely, softening the austere effect of its polished black surface by sheathing the walls in sea-foam-colored glass that glows from reflected light. The effect is like a grotto beneath a sun-dappled sea.

Solution Another hallway became a comfortable study (opposite) in the hands of designer David Kleinberg, who fitted a long shelf-*cum*-work-surface in the narrow space. By placing it opposite the wide opening to the adjacent living room, he gave the space an airiness that belies its tight dimensions; the window effect of the flat-screen television adds to the illusion. Boxes under the desk perform the mundane chore of hiding unsightly papers and supplies while an imposing statue adds the requisite glamour.

Belying its location in a Boston high-rise, this loftlike apartment is lined with cabinets and closets that keep the space open and free-flowing. In the bedroom area, architect Peter Forbes designed a compact enclosure that contains a study carrel behind folding doors that render it invisible when it's not in use. Vertical blinds control the light pouring through the floor-to-ceiling window. Minimalist modern accessories like the Mies van der Rohe chair and the Tizio lamp round out the refined environment.

The romance of a Paris garret was the aim when designer Anne Marie Vingo took on the task of turning space that was once servants' quarters into a home office. Because the room in this turn-of-the-century San Francisco house was not large, the question became where to put the desk and files without interfering with the abundant natural light or Gallic charm.

Solution Vingo constructed a cocoonlike work space in a former closet, outfitting it with built-in cabinets and shelves. Both the graceful Biedermeier chair and crisscrossed fabric strips that create the bulletin board hark back to the nineteenth century (left, below). A slim Neoclassical desk and klismos chair provide an alternate area for working (left, above)—or perhaps gazing out at the rooftop vista.

In a masterfully modernized Washington, D.C., home, a work area had to be constructed in the living room (above).

Solutions "If you can't beat 'em, join 'em" was the motto here. Rather than camouflage the space, designer Albert Hadley chose a bold oak console table with leather straps as an occasional work space and auxiliary storage for books. Topping it with a huge, attention-grabbing canvas, Hadley adroitly made the work area look as handsome as the rest of the room. In a guest room (opposite), an X-legged table became a design accent, serving as both writing surface and dressing table. Its curved lines are a graceful contast to the four-poster bed and 1950s-retro chairs.

Keep in mind If your work space must fit discreetly into another room, consider a handsome table rather than a traditional desk. Then position it for dramatic effect.

For those who want to separate the public and private areas in their home, bedrooms are often the first-choice location for work spaces. However, to do this successfully it is necessary to reduce the potential conflict between study and sleeping.

Solution A drop-lid desk is the easiest answer. When not in use, it closes to put work out of sight and, one hopes, out of mind. Designer Greg Jordan used this idea in two rooms of an upstate New York Greek Revival home. The prettily patterned master bedroom (above) takes to an American Chippendale example in mahogany. In the blue-and-white guest room (left), an eighteenth-century American fall-front desk is tucked neatly into a corner beside the fireplace. In both rooms, books are handily stacked on bedside chairs.

In a West Virginia mountain retreat, an airy sleeping loft has just enough corner space for a compact desk and built-in shelving (above). A screened porch is accessed through the adjacent door. Architect Mark McInturff designed the loft as part of a quirky, three-building complex, the polar opposite of his client's buttoned-up corporate office. Taking a more formal approach, designer Paul Wiseman engineered a hold-everything armoire that turns one wall of his eclectic San Francisco apartment into a work space and home entertainment center (opposite). Painted in a golden tone to match the room's boiserie paneling, it has a retractable writing surface and pull-out compartments for CDs. The George IV black-lacquer chair with chinoiserie decoration is a companion to the bedside chest.

For those daydreaming interludes, there's nothing so appealing as a desk in front of a window—but too much direct sunlight can be both distracting and uncomfortable. **Solution** A better idea, illustrated by designer William Hodgins in this gracious Palm Beach bedroom (opposite and above), is to set the desk perpendicular to the window wall, where it can benefit from maximum light with minimum glare, thanks also to adjustable louvers. The desk, a black-lacquered antique Empire writing table, has a single drawer—more than adequate storage for a second-home work space. Outfitted with a columnar lamp and curvy upholstered open armchair, it blends in comfortably with the room's classic tropical style.

A Japanese businesswoman with a taste for sparsely furnished spaces, Brian Stoner's client felt right at home in the coolly serene bedroom he incorporated into her Deco-style high-rise apartment in New York. A black-lacquered counter and custom-made seat allow the owner to work Asian style, close to the floor. Resting on traditional tatami mats, the futon is outfitted to face away from the window, allowing its occupant to focus on the calming interior.

PART THREE

Getting Down to Business

  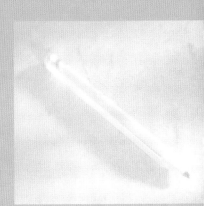

When you're setting up a home office, it's tempting to decorate first and put off practical considerations such as work surfaces, equipment, storage, sufficient light, and physical comfort. But no matter how attractive it looks, your home office won't be useful if it lacks any of the essentials. So before you begin making it pretty, make sure your office includes all these features.

First, a generous desk or work surface: It must be large enough to allow you to spread out papers or for whatever your work requires. It should be easy to clean, comfortable to lean on, and the right height for you. Desks are generally 28 to 30 inches tall; computer-keyboard shelves, 2 to 5 inches lower. If you lack room for two surfaces, you can buy a keyboard tray that mounts under a shelf or desktop and pulls out for use.

All work areas need some shelf space, but if you've accumulated lots of books for work, they may demand shelves that wrap around the room—a solution that can be as attractive as it is functional. In the home office of a food writer, open-back bookcases supply ample room for cookbooks without overpowering the space. To lighten the density of wall-to-wall books, the occasional shelf is left vacant for small pictures and other artwork. Appearing to float in a sea of pale oak flooring—another visual space stretcher—a 5-foot-long work table is supplemented with a custom-fitted unit that holds computer and keyboard, lighting, and roomy drawers.

A custom-built office would, of course, be perfect for everyone. But contrary to what one might think, it needn't be a major expense if the designer is clever.

Solution To keep costs down in her crisply contemporary Florida apartment, designer Alison Spear used simple wood to create the hold-everything unit for this bedroom. Painted white for the lightest possible look, the wall-wide piece serves as desktop, storage, and home entertainment center. Tiffany gift boxes add cachet without cost, holding knickknacks as they add a splash of their signature robin's-egg blue, while the black leather Pollack chair strikes a more corporate note.

Works well Inexpensive picture lights fit neatly under the ceiling, providing a low-key but attractive light source.

Since almost every type of business nowadays requires a computer, that's probably the first and most important piece of equipment you'll want to make room for. If you're short on surface space or prefer to have the computer out of sight when it's not in use, you might prefer a laptop, which when closed can fit into a cabinet or a drawer. Most desktop versions—even those that combine monitor and hard drive in one unit—are bulkier; you may want to look into the new space-saving flat-screen monitors and cordless mouse units. Other items such as printers, fax machines, and scanners may require additional countertop or shelf space, though they are also available in compact combination units. If your desk has multiple uses (dining table, kitchen counter), or it's a hinged, drop-down surface, consider placing the computer on a nearby shelf with access to an outlet or on a mobile workstation or pull-up table. If you like to work in bed, a laptop can rest where its name suggests or on a wheeled serving table that fits over the bed to hold it at a better angle. Just be certain you have enough light on the screen to prevent eyestrain.

Most home offices must accommodate a phone, perhaps one with multiple lines, and an answering machine. Add to this the need for "extras"—in-box, desk organizer, tape dispenser—and you may find that the simple little desk you envisioned has morphed into an eight-foot-long elephant. On the other hand, it's better to anticipate all this before you're beguiled by that charming eighteenth-century secretary that would nest perfectly in a bedroom corner but wouldn't hold more than the accoutrements for an afternoon of old-fashioned pen-and-paper correspondence.

Perhaps the hardest part of setting up a home office is finding space for the requisite wires and cables (and places to plug them all in; remember that you'll need sufficient power and outlets for lighting, too). If the resultant tangle of cords can't be recessed into a wall, concealed in hollow molding, or hidden behind a cabinet, you can tuck them into a plastic "cord caddy" for a neater look.

The chair is probably the most important purchase you will make for a home office—and the most problematic. Obviously, an ergonomically designed chair will offer the best possible support. Still, that may not be what you had in mind for the desk at one end of the living room or in the bedroom window bay. What's the best compromise? A choice that balances aesthetics and common sense. If you expect to spend hours at your desk, pick the most attractive ergonomic chair possible—there are many stylish models on the market— instead of seating that's easy on the eye but difficult to perch on for any length of time. Failing that, consider buying two chairs—one for work, and one for when company comes (and the office chair hides in a closet).

Lighting is generally the most neglected aspect of any home. It is even more critical in a work space. Eyestrain is not only physically taxing, it keeps you from working efficiently and can ultimately harm your vision. A rule of thumb: If you have to squint when you're working, you don't have enough light. A

H O M E / W O R K

How to Outfit Your Office
Five Must-Have Features

1. **A suitable work surface:** large enough for your needs, high enough to clear your knees (usually 28 to 30 inches)

2. **The right equipment:** computer and peripherals, telephone, fax machine, plus adequate and accessible outlets and sufficient electricity to run them

3. **Storage space:** shelves, drawers, or cabinets that can hold everything you need close at hand

4. **Good lighting:** Ambient light to illuminate the general area, and task lighting on the desktop or overhead to focus on your work

5. **Physical comfort:** an ergonomic chair, controlled heat and air-conditioning, perhaps a radio or CD player, minirefrigerator, teapot, or coffeemaker

When workaday needs must be met in a formally decorated home, the office furniture should measure up to its setting. In the eclectic, French-accented apartment of a New York City fashion journalist, a Louis XV lacquered desk and Italian Neoclassical chair set the stylish scene, underscoring a wall arrangement of fashion photographs and drawings by celebrity couturiers. A polished black-wood floor enhances the dressed-up look, while witty toss pillows and a leopard-skin seat cushion keep it all from becoming too serious.

You wouldn't expect to find a home office in a bathroom—but this is no ordinary bathroom (opposite). Designer Thomas O'Brien assembled this 660-square-foot fantasy from a rabbit warren of servants' quarters in a New York town house and equipped it with all the features of a luxury bathroom and sauna (not shown), plus an inviting sitting room and secluded work space. Avoiding the formula of white for bathrooms, he paved the floor in marble mosaic, then softened the effect with pale gray-green upholstered walls and muted lighting. A walnut-and-aluminum desk fits neatly into a corner, with papers confined to a white lacquer tray (overleaf, left), and French mid-twentieth-century club chairs offer a place to relax and read. An O'Brien-designed walnut cabinet with skyscraper silhouette provides stylish storage space (overleaf, right).

work area will usually have a combination of overall ambient light, adjustable task lights (preferably halogen), and, for decorative effect, accent lighting. The computer screen should be well lit, without glare, and light should not shine into your eyes. The best option in a windowed work area is to place the desk and computer perpendicular to the window, to allow for the changing direction of natural light during the course of the day.

Often forgotten, but absolutely necessary to a work space, is a congenial climate. The pleasure of having a desk by the window can be cancelled out by the discomfort of chilly drafts or an overheated radiator. In summer, an accessible air-conditioner—or, at least, a well-ventilated room—is essential to working comfort. Think of, and plan for, these quality-of-life requirements.

One of the most important office accessories is a wastebasket. Depending on the amount of paper you generate, you might want to invest in a paper shredder as well. And organizers—decorative in-and-out boxes, storage bins, and stacking storage units in patterned cardboard, lacquered wood, wicker, or colorful plastic—make it possible to outfit a desk handsomely while keeping it orderly.

Perhaps the ultimate indulgence is to equip your home office so that you needn't leave until your work is finished—coffeemaker, minirefrigerator, CD player, a couch or comfy chair for convenient breaks that don't lead you too far astray . . . .

If you've done everything according to plan, your home office should be just about perfect—or, more precisely, just perfect for you.

Freed from the constraints of a conventional business setting, a home office can express the owner's personal style. For furniture craftsman Daniel Hale, that meant eschewing typical office furniture in favor of something more fanciful for his easygoing Maryland home.

Solution Hale crafted this one-of-a-kind secretary and matching desk and decked them out with friendly faces, each one different. The drop-lid desk provides the perfect spot for perusing books.

Works well In the living area (above), chicken wire covers the country-style bookcase to help mask its less-than-neat contents.

In the Paris apartment of designer Michelle Halard, an idiosyncratic mix of vivid color and furniture styles imparts a Gallic panache to even the humblest pieces. A simple wood trestle table in a bedroom gains stature from the lushly draped tall windows, rose-colored walls and upholstery, and graceful Neoclassical-style seating (left). With a comfortable chair and good task lighting, it's within easy reach of the inviting clutter of books that fill the shelves Halard built, from floor to ceiling, along the opposite wall (above).

How can a traditional interior contain a contemporary-style work space? The high ceilings and strong architectural detailing of this nineteenth-century Paris apartment provided an elegant backdrop for designer Christian Liaigre. The challenge was to choose furniture that would be compatible in scale yet sleekly modern. Solution In the bedroom (left) an ebony-stained desk and chair created by Liaigre are striking contrasts to the crisp white walls and light wood herringbone floor. In the grand salon (opposite) a custom-designed library table in black lacquer and white oak is perfectly situated in front of an elaborately molded panel, which also frames a contemporary painting. Works well For work, the table, which converts to a dining surface, is decked out with simple ceramic and lacquer accessories and a convenient desktop light.

Whether it's a flea market find or a sleek new modern classic, almost any table can be pressed into service as a desk. Even the simplest Parsons table (above) can be both buffet counter and writing surface. Chinese wood-and-brass boxes that pick up the room's color scheme hold writing materials, while an egg-shape lamp sheds lots of light. In the corner of a New York City kitchen (opposite), the artist-occupant used a distressed, turned-leg table to create a cheerfully congested space that's handy for spur-of-the-moment sketching . . . and sneaked a tiny TV in, as well.

In each of these New York rooms the owners created the stately ambience of a European salon infused with their own personal styles. And each wanted work space that would blend seamlessly into the formal interior scheme. **Solution** In the town house parlor (above) designer Greg Jordan chose a French neoclassical desk to suit the Franco-Asian décor. At right angles to the wall, it gives the illusion of enclosure.

Solution Designer Noel Jeffrey played off the mostly modern furniture against the library's formal wood paneling (opposite). The austere oak desk is a provocative counterpoint to the built-in mahogany bookcases.

Reflecting the artistic pursuits and travels of the occupants, these his-and-her offices embody the working worlds of a married couple. In the writer husband's office (above), the desk is an old library table, battered but ample and lit by flanking floor lamps. Though his books are stacked high on every wall, apparently at random, he knows the precise location of each one. The office of his photographer wife (left) is a more idiosyncratic design mix: A clean-lined Robsjohn-Gibbings table is accompanied by fiberglass chairs from the 1962 Seattle World's Fair, and a pair of massive antique Chinese cabinets serves for all-purpose storage. Her art and photography books totter toward the ceiling atop the chests and in the corner. A Turkish carpet unifies the eclectic arrangement.

For serious collectors the work-at-home space should do more than provide a place for office supplies: it should also reflect the owner's art or design preferences. Solution The home office of a connoisseur of twentieth-century design (above) is appropriately furnished with classics of the period: a 1927 Paul Frankl skyscraper desk, a Gilbert Rohde chair and clock, and Machine Age accessories. The poster is a Lester Beall classic. For a couple who buys mostly French modern furniture, designer Michael Formica created a work area with a natural-wood desk and chair and Jean Royère branching floor lamp (opposite).

Glass, generally thought of as fragile, can be an excellent choice for a desktop. Except for the minor inconvenience of fingerprints, it's strong, comfortable to write on, and easy to clean. Its most appealing characteristic: Glass blends with any decor. In this chic living room, an Albrizzi-designed chrome trestle table with a smoked-glass top has a lightness of scale that belies its generous 60-inch length. Topped with a complementary chrome desk lamp, it holds a carefully arranged cluster of necessities and objets d'art.

To create a work area that does not look like an office, one needs a way to keep papers hidden.

Solution A hinged desktop mounted on a chest of drawers neatly solves the problem. We call the piece a secretary, the French named it the secretaire, and both names are derived from the Latin word for secret. For a pastel-pretty Palm Beach bedroom (left), designers James Aman and Anne Carson chose an eighteenth-century Swedish Gustavian version, whose pale painted finish flatters the silvery accessories. Cubbyholes and tiny drawers hold supplies. A white fall-front secretary in a print dealer's Boston Back Bay living room (opposite) plays a supporting role in the graphics-filled interior, complementing the gray-and-black palette.

To create a cozy library in her mostly open New York City loft, Venetian-trained designer Tiziana Hardy constructed economical bookshelves out of ordinary chipboard and lacquered them a rich blue. By staggering the shelves, she avoided the monotony of row upon row of volumes symmetrically placed. The design provided space for an ancestral double portrait above a Shaker-style country pine desk. Outfitted with comfortable seating, the library provides overflow space for parties.

The absence of clutter is a hallmark of most modern environments. So, how does one fit a work space into a minimalist environment?

Solution In an airy New Mexico living room (above), designer Joe D'Urso set out a pale-oak trestle table and left it almost bare. Papers hide in closed cabinets, while the built-in shelves hold a precise display of Native American artifacts.

Solution In an urbane city setting, a table-desk of light and black-stained oak sits before a backless bookcase of open cubes (opposite). Its geometric framework imposes a sense of order on the many small objects it contains.

A cozy arrangement like this may seem too informal for an office, but Los Angeles designer and inveterate entertainer Suzanne Rheinstein finds it the perfect work space for planning dinner parties. The desk is nothing more than a shelf mounted below the windows, broad enough for spreading out menus and invitation samples. Notes and family photos are tacked up on fabric-covered walls. Completing the laid-back mood are lounge chairs in an exuberant crewel-inspired print and wicker baskets for storage.

Because the world-traveler photographer who created this office in a Greenwich Village brownstone also uses it as a studio, the area often has to be cleared for photo shoots. One option might have been a small desk against the wall, but the owner did something more creative.

Solution He designed a cherry desk whose slender legs can be removed when space is needed for setups. Contributing to the room's feeling of openness are bare-plank floors and skinny metal chairs by Michael Formica. A casual arrangement of the artist's photographs, gilt-framed paintings, and fish trophy help personalize the space.

Works well An architect's angle-arm lamp clipped to one end allows for maximum work space, and can be removed in the blink of an eye.

To reflect the refined taste and personality of the owner, a high-powered female executive, Brian Stoner wanted to transform the living room of a conventional New York City high-rise apartment into something more visually commanding. But he had to make room for work space.

Solution Choosing a deco style, Stoner sculpted an undulating ceiling to create architectural interest in the boxy space and to act as a visual anchor for the furniture arrangement. A curved white-lacquer desk and shapely skirted chairs mark the work area of this seafoam-and-white haven, framed by double doors with frosted-glass squares that transmit lots of light.

Dressed for company, artist-craftsman Robert Bergero's Paris apartment looks like this, a mélange of eighteenth- and nineteenth-century styles mixing comfortably in the modest-size space that serves as both sitting room and atelier. Because the home is also his studio, it was necessary to hide equipment when visitors came to call. **Solution** A red-lacquered folding screen and caddy keep art materials out of sight. When Bergero wants to work on his handmade lamps and accessories he moves aside the vintage sycamore desk and sets up an ordinary wood trestle table. The quirky "twig" chair works well either way. **Why it works** Handsomely painted screens are marvelously effective for hiding clutter and, as shown here, also add a striking visual element.

Who would know this charming space is an office! Work brought home on the weekends should be done in peaceful surroundings. In his eighteenth-century weekend cottage in Connecticut, designer John Funt placed his bedroom office before unadorned windows, ensuring a front-row seat to view the greenery beyond. A nineteenth-century pine trestle table, in keeping with the exposed-beam folk-art stenciled interior, provides a sizeable writing surface.

Works well A comfy chaise, ready for reading either work documents or the Sunday paper, adds to the relaxed feel.

Despite the dictum that work areas should be tidy, it's hard in the midst of projects to put everything away. Not to worry.

Solution A pileup of objects can sometimes add considerable charm, as shown here. Stacks of storage boxes and books form an impromptu still life on the drop-leaf table designer Martine Colliander devised to serve as either desk (right) with one leaf raised, or dining table. In the green-walled Paris apartment of designer-retailer Patrice Gruffaz (opposite), family treasures and offbeat accessories meet in unexpected harmony. Dressed up in white paint, an old kitchen table makes a fine stand-in for a desk, accompanied by Restauration-style country chairs, resin sconces by Roberto Bergero, and witty Gruffaz-designed lamps.

Keep in mind Use storage boxes to contain clutter and office supplies. The more attractive the better, because they will add to—not subtract from—the décor.

Being fashionably eclectic without following any particular formula, designer Nancy Kitchell turned a rustic Mexican dining table into a work surface in her Arizona home (above), housing books and collections of what she describes as "peculiar things like old dice" in a tall pine cabinet. On the rear wall, wide, low shelves hold oversize volumes, and a thin clerestory window admits sunlight while minimizing glare. In a more citified setting (opposite), a crisp-edged rectangular table is placed console-style against a long wall for writing, playing games, and dining. Boxy rattan chairs echo the tropical flavor of the paneled screen mounted on the wall. Keep in mind Sometimes a big beautiful table to spread work out on is all you need.

When the need for work space is critical, almost any available surface will do as desktop. For a vacation house in San Miguel de Allende, Mexico, Michael Tracy outfitted a casually chic living room with a taller-than-usual wood-and-metal coffee table that's suitable for spreading out paperwork—though it's too low for comfort when working at a computer. The downside of an otherwise convenient work area such as this? Having to clear off the table before the guests arrive.

The most underutilized space in the home may be the dining room. Why let all that square footage go to waste when it can become a part-time office?

Solution In designer Christian Liaigre's Paris town house (above), the dark-stained dining table never languishes between mealtimes, and a back-less wall unit that displays artwork holds reference books as well, without making the room feel corporate. Taking a similar approach in a New York City apartment (opposite), designer Thomas O'Brien chose a striking gray-stained ash trestle table that serves as desk or dining surface.

Works well The versatile X-frame steel étagère can turn on its end—the shelves set in the other direction—to make a taller unit.

A photographer and collector of mid-century modern design needed lots of storage and work space in his New York City apartment. However, its dimensions were modest and he didn't want office equipment to overwhelm his prized collections.

Solution Embracing multipurpose efficiency, he took advantage of 14-foot ceilings, adding shelves atop existing bookcases that frame the windows and finishing them with molding for a unified look (left, above). Around the doorways, more shelves hold the owner's ever-growing collection of design books (left, below). In a corner of the living room, his passion for modern objects extends to the double-decker table (opposite), whose accessories include a vintage Walter von Nessen lamp and Ettore Sottsass's iconic typewriter.

The ideal home office, like any successful interior, is designed specifically for the owner's needs. In this case, the resident of a Manhattan loft wanted a work area that could also function as library and guest room. To ensure complete privacy, architect Walter Radke enclosed a section of the otherwise wide-open space to create a modern variation on the Renaissance *studiolo*, and designer Sabrina Schilcher outfitted it for shipshape style and efficiency. Maple shelves cover almost every inch of three walls, with upper levels accessed by a rolling ladder (opposite). Colored sliding panels cover storage areas. Just enough wall space was left free for the pickled-oak desk, paired with a biomorphic 1950s plywood chair. In the far corner (right), beneath "windows" that look onto the rest of the loft, low banquettes serve for sitting or sleeping.

Awkward spaces, well-designed, can have an offbeat appeal that conventional rooms lack. Witness a garden designer's very personal study and library (right, above and below) created in the attic of an upstate New York country home. Bookshelves, lining every wall up to the steeply raked ceiling, house an encyclopedic collection of garden books that can be enjoyed from a comfortable armchair or in bed. In the hearth-fitted kitchen (opposite), a plain-Jane wooden table between the windows provides auxiliary space for meal planning; nearby are narrow cases crammed with cookbooks.

Despite the risk of glare —and the distractions of a beautiful view—placing a desk in a window bay is sometimes too inviting to resist. Since the movie-star owner of this glamorous Beverly Hills home planned to use the work space only occasionally, designer Kerry Joyce faced the polished black desk toward the garden in the niche of a bright bedroom sitting area. When necessary, translucent white shades can be pulled down to subdue the California sun. Although it's massive, the well-proportioned storage unit doesn't look it, with glass doors on the upper section to lighten the effect.

Room for books and sundries can often be found in pieces intended for something altogether different. The answer is to appropriate pieces intended for something altogether different.

Solution In a nineteenth-century New Jersey farmhouse (above), designer Michael Maher and his antiques-dealer wife salvaged cabinets from a pantry; they now hold miscellany such as fabric samples, swatch books, and old magazines in a cozily casual home office. In the guest suite they built in an old stone house in Maine (opposite), decorators Mallory Marshall and James Light removed the ceiling of a top-floor room to expose the wood beams, then made them the crowning point for a wall of bookshelves. Guests can select a book, then continue up the ladder to a sleeping loft.

This elegant arrangement has all the essentials of a home office: a surface to write on, a chair to sit on, a place to put books and papers, and enough light to see what you're doing. The owner, architect William Ellis, designed the combination desk-drafting table-flat file and matching storage tray. The built-in shelves are adjustable, a wise choice for anyone with a large collection and limited space. They can be set at the precise height necessary to accommodate volumes large or small without wasting precious inches. For task lighting, the metal lamp with articulated arm is one of the most effective models.

Directory and Index of Designers and Architects

James Aman & Anne Carson
Aman & Carson, Inc. (132)
New York, NY
(212) 794-8878

Thomas M. Beeton &
    Associates, Inc. (24)
Los Angeles, CA
(310) 657-5600

Roberto Bergero (144)
Paris, France
011-33-1-42-72-03-51

Woody Biggs
Paris Prints
Sausalito, CA
(415) 289-0529

Cynthia Butler (85)
Insight Interior Corp.
New York, NY
(212) 366-6413

Jack DeBartolo, Jr. (48)
DeBartolo Architects
Phoenix, AZ
(602) 264-6617
www.debartoloarchitects.com

Peter de Bretteville
    Architects (41)
New Haven, CT
(203) 785-0586

Tony Cantalini (30)
Cantalini Associates
Oakland, CA
(510) 444-5335
Palm Desert, CA
(760) 341-7737
www.cantalini.com

Monte Coleman
New York, NY
(212) 463-0085

Martine Colliander (149)
Solgården Collection
    from Lexington Furniture
(800) 539-4636
www.lexington.com

Celeste Cooper (53)
Repertoire
Boston, MA
(617) 426-3865
New York, NY
(212) 219-8159
www.repertoire.com

T. Keller Donovan, Inc. (69)
New York, NY
(212) 760-0596

Robin Dripps &
    Lucia Phinney (69)
Architecture & Urbanism
Batesville, VA
(434) 823-4969

Steven Ehrlich Architects (60)
Culver City, CA
(310) 838-9700
www.s-ehrlich.com

William Ellis, Architect (167)
New York, NY
(212) 639-1377

Peter Forbes, FAIA,
    Architects (92)
Seal Harbor, ME
(207) 276-0970
Florence, Italy
011-39-055-462-7457

Ken Foreman (79)
Foreman Interior Designs
New York, NY
(212) 924-4503

Michael Formica, Inc. (128)
New York, NY
(212) 620-0655
www.michaelformica.com

Richard Gluckman
Gluckman Mayner Architects
New York, NY
(212) 929-0100

Mariette Himes Gomez (46)
Gomez Associates, Inc.
New York, NY
(212) 288-6856
www.mariettehimesgomez.com

Patrice Gruffaz
Paris, France
011-33-1-42-78-57-71

Albert Hadley, Inc. (96)
New York, NY
(212) 888-7979

Michelle Halard (119)
Paris, France
011-33-1-44-07-14-00

Amanda Halstead (56)
Halstead Designs
    International
New York, NY
(212) 879-1090

Tiziana Hardy (134)
New York, NY
(212) 777-5612

Laura Hartman (55)
Fernau & Hartman Architects
Berkeley, CA
(510) 848-4480
www.fernauhartman.com

William Hodgins, Inc. (87,103)
Boston, MA
(617) 262-9538

Kathryn Ireland
Santa Monica, CA
(310) 315-4351

Noel Jeffrey, Inc. (19, 124)
New York, NY
(212) 935-7775

Greg Jordan, Inc. (99, 124)
New York, NY
(212) 570-4470

Kerry Joyce Associates, Inc.
 (162)
Los Angeles, CA
(323) 938-4442
www.kerryjoyce.com

Nancy Kitchell (150)
Kitchell Interior Design
 Associates
Scottsdale, AZ
(480) 951-0280

David Kleinberg Design
 Associates (90)
New York, NY
(212) 754-9500

David Lake (64)
Lake/Flato Architects, Inc.
San Antonio, TX
(210) 227-3335

Max Levy Architect (34)
Dallas, TX
(214) 368-2023

Christian Liaigre (74, 155)
Holly Hunt
New York, NY
(212) 755-6555
www.hollyhunt.com

Vico Magistretti (72)
Milan, Italy
011-39-02-7600-2964

Michael Maher (164)
New York, NY
(212) 744-0120

Nancy Mannucci, ASID
New York, NY
(212) 427-9868

Mallory Marshall &
 James Light (164)
Mallory James Interiors
Portland, ME
(207) 773-0180
www.malloryjames.com

Mark McInturff (100)
McInturff Architects
Bethesda, MD
(301) 229-3705

Katherine McCallum (88)
McMillen, Inc.
New York, NY
(212) 753-5600

Herman Miller for the Home
(800) 646-4400
www.hermanmiller.com

Lee S. Mindel, FAIA (79)
Shelton, Mindel & Assoc.
New York, NY
(212) 243-3939

Thomas O'Brien (112, 155)
Aero Studios, Ltd.
New York, NY
(212) 966-4700
www.aerostudios.com

Walter Radtke (159)
New York, NY
(212) 460-5253

Suzanne Rheinstein &
 Associates (139)
West Hollywood, CA
(310) 550-8900

Rockwell Group
New York, NY
(212) 463-0334
www.rockwellgroup.com

Sabrina Schilcher (159)
Salon Moderne
New York, NY
(212) 219-3439

Stephen Shubel Design, Inc.
Ross, CA
(415) 925-9332

Sharon Simonaire Design, Inc.
 (13)
New York, NY
(212) 242-1824

Alison Spear, AIA (168)
New York, NY
(212) 439-8506
www.alisonspearaia.com

Kate Stamps (70)
Stamps & Stamps
South Pasadena, CA
(626) 441-5600

Brian Stoner (90, 104, 142)
New York, NY
(212) 757-0369

Michael Tracy (152)
San Ygnacio, TX
(956) 765-4144

Calvin Tsao & Zack
 McKown
Tsao & McKown Architects
New York, NY
(212) 337-3800

Turnbull Griffin Haesloop
 (66)
Berkeley, CA
(415) 986-3642
www.tgharchs.com

Priscilla Ulmann (88)
Scott-Ulmann, Inc.
Southampton, NY
(631) 259-0280

Ann Marie Vingo (94)
 Interior Design
San Francisco, CA
(415) 776-7555

Kelly Wearstler
KWID
Los Angeles, CA
(323) 951-7454

Matthew White Interior
 Design (20)
Pasadena, CA
(626) 403-1730
www.matthewwhitedesign.com

Paul Wiseman (100)
The Wiseman Group Interior
 Design, Inc.
San Francisco, CA
(415) 282-2880
www.wisemangroup.com

Photography Credits

1–2	Jonn Coolidge
5	Dominique Vorillon
6–7	Jonn Coolidge
9	Paul Whicheloe
12	Oberto Gili
15–17	Jonn Coolidge
18–19	Pieter Estersohn
20–23	David Phelps
24–27	John Ellis
28–29	Eric Boman
30–31	David Duncan Livingston
32–33	Quentin Bacon
34–35	Scott Frances
36–37	Jon Jensen
38–39	Timothy Hursley
40–43	Scott Frances
44–45	Jon Jensen
46–47	Thibault Jeanson
48–49	Timothy Hursley
50–51	William Waldron
52–53	Peter Margonelli
54	Peter Aaron/Esto
57	Tom McWilliam
58	Jonn Coolidge
61	Tim Street-Porter
62	Eric Roth
63	Richard Felber
64–65	Timothy Hursley
66	Scott Frances
67	Minh & Wass
68	Robert Lautman
69	Gabi Zimmerman
70–71	Tim Street-Porter
72–73	Santi Caleca
74–75	Jacques Dirand
76–77	Fernando Bengoechea
78	Jonn Coolidge
79	Peter Margonelli
80–81	Herman Miller for the Home
82–83	Oberto Gili
84–85	Paul Whicheloe
86–87	Tim Beddow
88–89	Jeff McNamara
90	William Waldron
91	Fernando Bengoechea
92–93	William Waldron
94–95	Jon Jensen
96–97	Oberto Gili
98–99	Fernando Bengoechea
100	Robert Lautman
101	Tim Street-Porter
102–103	Jacques Dirand
104–105	William Waldron
106	Christopher Irion
109	Michael Weschler
110	Fernando Bengoechea
113–115	Laura Resen
116–117	Jeff McNamara
118–119	Thibault Jeanson
120–121	Jacques Dirand
122	Alex McClean
123	Minh & Wass
124	Thibault Jeanson
125	Scott Frances
126–127	Laura Resen
128	John Hall
129	Robert Hiemstra
130–131	Susie Cushner
132	Scott Frances
133	Thibault Jeanson
134–135	Scott Frances
136	Oberto Gili
137	Thibault Jeanson
138–139	Tim Street-Porter
140–141	Oberto Gili
142–143	William Waldron
144–145	Erica Lennard
146–147	William Waldron
148	René Stoeltie
149	Jonn Coolidge
150–151	Jacques Dirand
152–153	Hickey-Robertson
154	Laura Resen
155	Jacques Dirand
156–157	John M. Hall
158–159	Paul Whicheloe
160–161	Richard Felber
162–163	William Waldron
164	Laura Resen
165	Wiliam Waldron
166–167	Laura Resen
169	Robert Hiemstra
170	Oberto Gili
173	Tim Beddow
174–175	Laura Resen
front case	Jonn Coolidge
back case	David Phelps

The room on page 1 was designed by Lee S. Mindel; page 2, Kelly Wearstler; page 5, Stephen Shubel and Woody Biggs; pages 6–7, Calvin Tsao and Zack McKown; page 9, Nancy Mannucci; page 169, Michael Formica and Richard Gluckman; page 170, Albert Hadley; page 173, Kathryn Ireland; pages 174–175, Monte Coleman.

Index

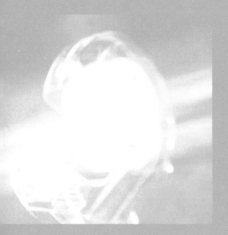